THIS NORTHERN LAND

Devenish Island, Co. Fermanagh

Alf McCreary

Christopher Hill

THIS NORTHERN LAND

GREYSTONE BOOKS

encouraged me a great deal as a boy, but he later felt that full-time photography was not a secure career. My first six years were very tough, but I survived."

Chris Hill gradually built up a reputation as a first-class professional with a flair for photography over a wide range of subjects. His credo is simple: "The essence of a good photographer is to have an 'eye' and to know the capabilities and limitations of the camera." Yet there is something more that is required, a quality which he illustrates indirectly when he describes the picture of the Giant's Causeway, on the front of this book. He had gone to the North Antrim Coast to photograph the dusk and the dawn, and to sleep overnight in his car between taking pictures. "The shots of dusk were not very promising, so I decided to get something to eat. I switched on my car's headlights which shone directly on to the Causeway, and the picture I saw is exactly what you see on the cover of this book. That's what I mean by 'different'. Even though it was getting dark, I knew that I could balance the lights in a way that would give the Causeway a whole new feeling. That was a very exciting moment for me."

There are other striking and highly individual photographs in this volume, including a ploughed field near Cookstown, a study of Crawfordsburn Beach, a wooded glade at Armagh, a silhouette of Dunluce Castle, a fiery dawn over Whitepark Bay, and many others. He explains, "This collection is about light rather than people. It's about landscapes, and light on landscapes, about the moods of the countryside, and the hidden beauties. I hope that these pictures will make people stop and look and say to themselves, 'I wish I'd seen that'. In all probability they have, but they were possibly too unaware or too busy to take it in properly and to appreciate it."

As a writer, with a long experience of travelling the highways and byways of Ulster, I admire greatly Chris Hill's work, and I appreciate his "different" eye which can make a familiar scene appear quite new and refreshing. It has been both a privilege and a challenge to follow Chris on his journeys throughout "This Northern Land" and to try to match his moods with my own observations, based on an equally deep love of Ulster and its ways, and also to include some of the mood-setting prose and poetry from a number of my favourite writers.

In a strange way I have felt as if the pen and camera on this journey were like a soloist and orchestra, each blending and leading the following, for the benefit of the whole. If this blending of the pen and the camera has indeed produced something different for the eye and the understanding of the reader, then Chris Hill and I will both feel richly rewarded.

Alf McCreary
26 September 1989

WATER

Craigavon Lakes, Co. Armagh

N

"I see the waves upon the shore,
Like light dissolved in star-showers, thrown."

The poet Shelley moves between light and water with
an eye for beauty and with a deep understanding of the
nature of things. His awareness is much more penetrating
than the crisp, yet soulless, definition of "Water" in the
Oxford Dictionary– "colourless transparent tasteless
scentless compound of oxygen and hydrogen in liquid
state convertible by heat into steam and by cold into ice,
kinds of liquid consisting chiefly of this seen in sea, lake,
stream, spring, rain, tears, sweat, saliva . . ." and so on.

Water is all of this, and yet it is much more. The
writer–poet Laurie Lee in his immortal "Cider With
Rosie" relays with starry-eyed wonder his discovery of
water, as a child. "You could pump it in pure blue gulps
out of the ground, you could swing on the pump handle
and it came out sparkling like liquid sky. And it broke and
ran and shone on the tiled floor, or quivered in a jug, or
weighted your clothes with cold. You could drink it, draw

River Lagan, Co. Antrim

Glenoe, Co. Antrim

with it, froth it with soap, swim beetles across it, or fly it in bubbles in the air. You could put your head in it, and open your eyes, and see the sides of the bucket buckle, and hear your caught breath roar, and work your mouth like a fish, and smell the lime from the ground. Substance of magic – which you could wear or tear, confine or scatter, or send down holes, but never burn or break or destroy."

Indeed it is a "substance of magic", as described by a writer with almost magical powers of observation and communication. And although few can match Laurie Lee's prose, in a lifetime of writing, most of us have caught our own personal glimpses of the beauty, the diversity, and the power of Water. It is as much a part of life as breathing or eating. Water is sustenance and cleansing, transport and energy, re-creation and relaxation, comfort and catalyst, and, in its times of terrifying force, both dangerous and desolate.

Water was one of the most basic elements known to primitive man. It harboured food and provided refreshment. It irrigated land, and in its absence, crops withered and died. Water offered opportunities to cross vast tracts, to colonise new lands and to subjugate peoples. It helped to bring Bibles and diseases and skills and slaves to the New World, and in return to ferry riches and the objects of conquest and barter to the Old. It played a major part in diffusing whole cultures and in shaping the ebb and flow of history. It was water which bore the frail craft of Columba from Ireland to Iona in the outreach of Christianity, and it was water which equally sustained the Vikings in their conquests. Whole empires and civilisations drew their strength from the Waters as well as their people. Even today, historians and geographers with a global view talk about the decline of the "Age of the Atlantic" and look to the already dawning "Age of the Pacific".

Water, like Light, has a symbolic significance which is also deeply spiritual. The writer of Ecclesiastes implores; "Cast thy bread upon the waters: for thou shalt find it after many days." And the Prayer Book of 1662 intones:

"O ye Waters that be above the Firmament, bless ye the Lord.
. . . O ye Whales and all that move in the Waters,
bless ye the Lord: praise him and magnify him for ever."

On a much more humble level, Water has provided sport for countless small boys and the young-at-heart with a sapling for a rod, a bent pin for a hook, and a struggling worm for bait. Many an energetically lazy day has been spent profitably beside pond or stream, as the Waters gave up their secrets in the shape of slippery, silvery, slithering prey. Izaak Walton described better than any man the lure of fishing –"We may say of angling as Dr Boteler said of strawberries 'Doubtless God could have made a better berry, but doubtless God never did', and so,

Dunfanaghy, Co. Donegal

Narrow Water, Co. Down

Newcastle, Co. Down

I slip, I slide, I gloom, I glance,
Among my skimming swallows;
I make the netted sunbeam dance
Against my sandy shallows.

I murmur under moon and stars
In brambly wildernesses;
I linger by my shingly bars;
I loiter by my cresses;

And out again I curve and flow
To join the brimming river,
For men may come and men may go,

but I go on for ever."

At Newcastle the calm Waters of the lake, and the necklace of small, blue hulls all neatly strung together, belie the boisterous days of boating holidays and the raucous whistles and throaty cries of "Come on in, Number Seven, and Five, and Ten, and Eleven, and Three and Four . . . your time's up!" All of this is far removed from the stately white creature in the background which surely must be The Swan of W.R. Rodgers . . .

"Jonquil-long its neck adjudicates
Its body's course; aloof and cool
It cons the nonchalant and unseeing air
With its incurious and dispassionate stare

Slow, slow, it slides, as if not to chafe
The even sleeve of its approach
Stretched stiff and oval in front of it
Siphoning it on, selfless, silent and safe."

The appeal and power of Water surges through that almost mystic dawn which is pictured over Whitepark Bay. Did Neolithic Man, who all those millennia ago took the flint from the chalk to make arrowheads and tools, witness such Water and such fiery dawns? And in the peace of Ballygawley Lake, with nothing more fiery than the red roof of a wooden shack blending amid the colours, the mists across the still Water provide a study in serenity itself. This is almost the land of William Butler Yeats, with his search for peace in that Lake Isle of Innisfree and that yearning for "lake water lapping with low sounds by the shore."

The elemental fascination with water is indeed in that "deep heart's core" of all of us.

N

"Mountains are the beginning and the end of all natural scenery"

These words of John Ruskin place uplands and mountains in their proper perspective. There is a strength, a majesty and a challenge about hills which no other part of the natural landscape can match. There is no mistaking the primal instinct of man in looking upwards for renewed strength. "I will lift up mine eyes unto the hills, from whence cometh my help".

These words from Psalm 121 touch a deep well of universal need, even among those people who do not usually read the Bible. And in a less lofty but equally comforting and homespun way, the poet John Masefield captures the steadfastness of the uplands, in his description of "The West Wind":

> *"It's a warm wind, the west wind, full of birds' cries;*
> *I never hear the west wind but tears are in my eyes.*
> *For it comes from the west lands, the old brown hills,*
> *And April's in the west wind, and daffodils."*

Mourne Mountains, Co. Down

Roe Valley, Co. Londonderry

The uplands are wild places, the territory of the sheep and the syklark, and the swift brown fox scurrying amid heather and granite. Here too are the higher reaches of silence, where a man can be alone but not lonely, where the only suggestion of another living creature is the faint call of bird-sound carrying on the wind. This lonesome strength of the high places is reflected in the 19th century observation of the Reverend Francis Kilvert; "It is a fine thing to be out on the hills alone. A man can hardly be a beast or a fool alone on a great mountain." And the almost magical quality of the silence and strength in the hills is reflected by William Blake:

"Great things are done when men and mountains meet;
This is not done by jostling in the street."

Geographers, not surprisingly, take a rather more prosaic view. But there is re-assurance and even a hint of artistic appreciation in this accurate and restrained description of mountains by James Cruickshanks, a former Senior Lecturer in geography at the Queen's University of Belfast; "In Northern Ireland there are few mountains, but often they have a striking appearance in the landscape by virtue of their isolated position. Only 6 per cent of the total land area is above 300 m or 1,000 ft, but the mountains are distributed in isolated blocks peripheral to the central lowland, giving them a dominance over the surrounding landscape that belies their areal extent. The location of the Mountains of Mourne and the Antrim plateau cliffs adjacent to the coastline allows these mountains to rise high above the shore, and to provide a lasting impression in the mind of the traveller arriving by sea." Yet there is more to mountains than their geological dissection into "Tertiary granites and micha-schists", or "Carboniferous Limestone, Old Red Sandstone and Antrim Basalts." There are also the mountainy creatures, like the ram gazing with almost-regal splendour across the turbulent and treacherous waters off Fair Head, near Ballycastle. And there are the mountainy people who keep themselves to themselves but who move out of their relative isolation from time to time to become part of the structured hubbub of fair and mart, or to sink pints in the snug of a pub on a Saturday night. There are big men and craggy men, men with broad smiles and pinched faces, and big boots and cloth caps, men of wiry build and strong grips, of measured words and keen observations, the men of all winds and all weathers.

The Ulster poet John Hewitt knew such men and wrote with intimate knowledge about those country communities which are still close-knit to the soil. And yet in The Ram's Horn he looked beyond mankind, to something deeper, something without the disappointment that is part of the human condition:

> *"Animal, plant, or insect, stone or water,*
> *are, every minute, themselves; they behave by law.*
> *I am not required to discover motives for them,*
> *or to strip my heart to forgive the rat in the straw.*
>
> *I live my best in the landscape, being at ease there;*

> *the only trouble I find I have brought in my hand.*
> *See, I let it fall with a rustle of stems in the nettles,*
> *and never for a moment suppose that they understand."*

Landscape and uplands have a life of their own. They have surprises, too, like the sudden rush of water at Roe Valley, Limavady, or an engagingly different view of an industrial city across the mists leading to the Cave Hill, or even the sweep of a dappled herd behind a stone wall at Broughshane, Co. Antrim, showing the innate beauty in the most simple scenes and sights of everyday life. There is beauty, too, in the picture of a hard frost at Plumbridge, Co. Tyrone.

The abiding grandeur of the uplands lingers in the Mountains of Mourne in all their many moods and guises. They dominate but not obliterate, they tower but also blend. They are part of a larger landscape but they are also, in their crannies and corners and lesser peaks, country intimates sustaining and shaping a way of life for generations. That celebrated traveller H.V. Morton saw

Newcastle, Co. Down

N

"It is interesting to contemplate an entangled bank, clothed with many plants of many kinds, with birds singing on the bushes, with various insects flitting about, and with worms crawling through the damp earth, and to reflect that these elaborately constructed forms, so different from each other, and dependent upon each other in so complex a manner, have all been produced by laws acting around us . . . Growth with Reproduction; Inheritance . . . Variability . . . a Ratio of Increase so high as to lead to a Struggle for Life, and as a consequence to Natural Selection, entailing Divergence of Character and the Extinction of less-improved forms."

These observations by Charles Darwin in "The Origin of Species" provide a much less poetic theory of Man's beginning than, say, the Book of Genesis. And yet the evolution of Man has exhibited, at his very best, some remarkable qualities and skills of creativity which are reminiscent of that lofty and flowing description from the Prayer Book of 1662; "Thou madest him lower than the angels: to crown him with glory and worship".

Lisbane Post Office, Co. Down

No mortal eye could see
The intimate welding of their later history,

Or sign that they were bent
By paths coincident
On being twin halves of one august event . . .

Till the Spinner of the Years
Said 'Now!' And each one hears,
And consummation comes, and jars two hemispheres."

The huge cranes at Belfast shipyard are more than imprints. Like the Giant's Ring they are a monument to an entire way of life.

So too is Dunluce Castle perched high on its cliff-base at the North Antrim coast and witnessing to a stirring history long forgotten. In its brooding, bleak beauty there is a silent reminder to a wealth of derring-do, of power-struggles between local chieftains and their enemies, of violence, treachery and drama. There were nights of merry-making too, and of sudden death, most notably when the castle was full of guests and suddenly a part of the kitchen collapsed into the ocean, carrying with it a number of servants. Not far along the coast the Spanish Armada vessel, the Girona, foundered in October 1588 with heavy loss of life. Just as the beautiful and elaborate Escorial Palace, near the mountains north of Madrid, is a fascinating memorial to the austere King Philip II of Spain, who helped to set the Armada on its way, Dunluce Castle is part of that history which has come full circle.

There is history too in the rugged ruins of Downhill Castle, etched along the skyline like some stately pile in Italy or France. This was the former residence of the eccentric, yet with hindsight the enlightened, Frederick Augustus Hervey, the 4th Earl of Bristol and Bishop of Derry. He inspired the construction of Downhill Castle, which was completed in 1780. The Bishop was larger than life in an age when men of wealth made their mark on the history of their times. The Bishop was an inveterate traveller and art collector, and Downhill in its prime housed one of the greatest private art collections in Ire-

Mountstewart, Co. Down

land. Sadly, a later fire destroyed many of its treasures. Hervey was a man of the church, an ecumenist long before the word had been invented, and also a man of the world. He built the architecturally striking Mussenden Temple, still dominating the sweep of Downhill Strand, and named it after his beautiful female cousin, thereby scandalising some of his contemporaries who thought this most improper behaviour for a Bishop whose wife had recently left him. But Hervey had style, and that style is still apparent in his very personal imprints on the North coast. It is said that his motto, when constructing an Anglican church, was deceptively simple, "Let it decorate the country". Downhill Castle, though roofless and rather forlorn today, and the Mussenden Temple, bring to modern generations the mark of a man whose imprints are unmistakeable.

There are other imprints of men of means and of reputation in "This Northern Land". Lord Castlereagh, the British Foreign Secretary during the Napoleonic Wars, grew up at Mount Stewart in County Down and the visitor to this grand house will find all kinds of imprints, from some of the chairs used at the 1815 Congress of Vienna to the oustanding gardens with their strange collection of statues, including griffins, heraldic lions and other creations.

At Springhill in County Tyrone there is another distinctive imprint of a different way of life and of the survival of a Planter family and their descendants in the Mid-Ulster of the 17th and 18th Centuries, down to the warning-bell and gun-slits in the barn walls which characterised the defences of such hardy settlers in the not-so-friendly Province of their time. Over at Barnett's Park in Belfast there is Malone House, an elegant late Georgian mansion, which was built in the 1820's for a William Wallace Legge, a prominent Belfast merchant. The house was presented to the City of Belfast in 1946 by William Barnett, a local businessman, and is now a restaurant and a centre for conferences and exhibitions. It retains a sense of quiet beauty and spaciousness, with a marvellous view of the surrounding hills and countryside.

Facing page: Downhill, Co. Londonderry

For an island people it is difficult to contemplate a world where the sea is not within striking distance of a two-hours' journey or more. Those who live land-locked at the heart of continents may find attractions in their own local beauty, but anyone who has spent a childhood or half a lifetime near the sea would miss, in the depths of the soul, the ebb and flow of the tides, the cries of sea-birds, the beauty of a sunset over the ocean, and the almost cleansing effect of a blowy day beside a high sea where the cobwebs of life are tossed far across the tumbling waves. The sounds of the sea, whether lapping on the shore or roaring against cliff-face and inlet, are part of a vast symphony with infinite sub-themes moving around a strong and unchanging central core.

The sea is beauty, majesty, transport, recreation and refreshment, but it is also danger. It commands and demands respect, and even in an age of the most breathtaking technology and of impressive aids to safety, there are the continual and distressing stories of death and destruction at sea, whether the considerable loss of life in an oil-rig explosion or the capsize of a large, modern passenger vessel, or the individual tragedies of a boating trip, or a fishing expedition or an hour of swimming in high summer, all of which went badly wrong. Even in the midst of a glowing sunset over calm waters there is always in the back of the mind a remembrance of the awesome power of the sea and an awareness of those lines of William Whiting:

"O hear us when we cry to Thee
For those in peril on the sea."

Despite the dangers, the delights of sea and sea-side remain, perhaps encouraged by the bucket-and-spade holidays of youth on literally golden beaches long before European travel was possible for the mass of the people. And for the city-bound, and those who have to earn their living in the greyer terrain of towns and terraced streets, there is perhaps a dream of retiring, some day, to a little cottage or bungalow near the coast, and to echo the words

Facing page: Newcastle, Co. Down

66

Dundrum Bay, Co. Down

Carrick-a-Rede, Co. Antrim

might try to sound a little like Jonathan Livingston Seagull, surely one of the most famous and most impressive sea-birds of all . . .

"He learned more each day. He learned that a stream-lined high-speed dive could bring him to find the rare and tasty fish that schooled ten feet below the surface of the ocean, he no longer needed fishing boats and stale bread for survival. . . . What he had once hoped for the Flock, he now gained for himself alone; he learned to fly, and was not sorry for the price that he had paid. Jonathan Seagull discovered that boredom and fear and anger are the reasons that a gull's life is so short, and with these gone from his thought, he lived a long, fine life indeed."

This is an extremely wise and a philosophical Seagull, by any standards! Perhaps there can be too much gentle philosophy about the sea which, in its angry moods, as in the picture at Newcastle, can be troubled and treacher-ous. The sea, at heart, is a wild thing, and never to be taken for granted. But after the storm, there is the calm and the gentle light dipping from the cloud-base onto the sea, as at Glenarm. This could even be the scene from Tennyson's "Crossing the Bar":

"Sunset and evening star,
And one clear call for me!
And may there be no moaning of the bar
When I put out to sea."

In such an elegiac mood, the calm scene of beauty of the Antrim Coast, from Carrick-a-Rede, is a fitting ending to a sea symphony of lights and shades, of gentleness and of power, and of a deep respect so fittingly and poetically portrayed in the words of Psalm 107:

"They that go down to the sea in ships, that do business in
great waters;
These see the works of the Lord, and his wonders in the deep."

Facing page: Glenarm, Co. Antrim

Centuries later these words live on, just as the contours of Slemish itself remain largely unchanged. There is a timelessness, also, in the picture of the wheatfield in County Londonderry. James Turner, in his poem "Combine Harvester", captures the long ripening, and the inevitable, crushing end;

> *"All summerlong agrowing, green shoot*
> *To ripening, eager and sunswelled,*
> *To be consumed by cropping spikes,*
> *Devoured and threshed, divided*
> *In dark night of iron womb*
> *To corngrain and springstraw."*

The contrast and colours, and the strong light, of the countryside, create visual poetry amid the wonder of ordinary things, like a long vista of vegetables at Scrabo or the sharp green and yellows in a County Antrim rapefield. It is little wonder that Gerard Manley Hopkins, who had the soul's-eye for simple things, could write blazingly:

> *"The world is charged with the grandeur of God*
> *It will flame out like shining from shook foil."*

There is simple grandeur also in the picture of a ploughed field near Cookstown, with the drills as straight as Irish Guardsmen, stretching to the very skyline. Maybe it was just such a field which inspired W.R. Rodgers to write:

> *"I remember a small field in Down, a field*
> *Within fields, shaped like a triangle.*
> *I could have stood and looked at it*
> *All day long."*

The broad sweep and colour and contrast of the countryside is well-captured, too, by the curves of flax-cutting at Seaforde and by the rhododendron petals caressing the tree-trunks' base at Rowallane. There is something to stir the soul and to quicken the visual senses in a countryside so beautifully rich and varied as "This Northern Land".

Facing page: Rowallane, Co. Down

carol service where old Johnny Black read one of the lessons, and the village schoolmaster recited a poem, and everyone sang "Silent Night" while the Christmas tree twinkled near the altar. It was cosy in church, but outside it was cold under the stars, with the breath freezing in the chill evening air. Perhaps there might even be snow this year, and maybe – O, joy of joys, – a white Christmas!

The poet Dylan Thomas remembered his "A Child's Christmas in Wales", or did he? He wrote "I can never remember whether it snowed for six days and six nights when I was twelve, or whether it snowed for twelve days and twelve nights when I was six." But Laurie Lee, as ever, had remarkably clear recall when describing Christmas carolling in his boyhood village in the Cotswolds: "We grouped ourselves round the farmhouse porch. The sky cleared, and broad streams of stars ran down over the valley and away to Wales. On Slad's white slopes, seen through the black sticks of its woods, some red lamps burned in the windows.

"Everything was quiet; everywhere there was the faint crackling silence of the winter night. We started singing, and we were all moved by the words and the sudden trueness of our voices. Pure, very clear, and breathless we sang:

> *"As Joseph was walking*
> *He heard an angel sing:*
> *This night shall be the birth-time*
> *Of Christ the Heavenly King . . .*

"And two thousand Christmases became real to us then; the houses, the halls, the places of paradise had all been visited; the stars were bright to guide the Kings through the snow: and across the farmyard we could hear the beasts in their stalls. We were given roast apples and hot mince-pies, in our nostrils were spices like myrhh, and in our wooden box, as we headed back to the village, there were golden gifts for all."

Not everyone takes such a romantic view of winter or of Christmas, that originally pagan festival which the

Beech trees, Minnowburn, near Belfast